the death of Christmas

Fischetti

THE OUTSIDERS

the death of Christmas

Kenan Heise and Arthur Allan

ISBN 0-695-80274-7

Foreword

"Last year I had seven dollars to buy Christmas with."

The speaker, a mother of five, epitomizes the Christmas dilemma faced each year by thousands of Chicagoans and by millions of other Americans living below what we so glibly call "the poverty level"—as if by giving it a name we could erase the problem.

This dilemma consists of trying to create the appearance of Christmas for their children without having the substance—of making one scraped-up dollar do the work of fifty. And it is compounded by the fact that everyone's Christmas now, no matter where he clings to the social scale, must be compared with the Christmas shown on the television screen and in the newspaper and magazine advertisements, a Christmas blown up into a billion dollar business promotion by those who exploit the birthday of the Holy Child.

The pages which follow were put together by two

young Chicagoans who are old-fashioned enough to believe that Christmas should be more a thing of the spirit than the bankroll and that the ringing of church bells still is a lovelier sound than the tinkling of the cash register. Kenan Heise, who runs Action Line for *Chicago Today,* and Arthur Allan, Director of Public Relations for the Cook County Department of Public Aid, decided to find out what the Yuletide means to the drifter and the down-and-out, the harried mother on welfare, the inmates of the County jail, the old and the lonely. They asked questions, heard the replies, and this book is what happened.

It is a book filled with haunting phrases and broken hearts, yet it also somehow manages to be a book in which hope refuses to die completely. It suggests in ways too subtle to analyze that Christmas yet may return to those simpler and less jaded times when it still lacked the price-tags and the frenetic hullabaloo with which it now is surrounded.

Here is a sampling of what this slim survey of the modern Christmas has to offer:

"That year I bought a lot of gifts. My mom told me all the gifts I bought were wrong . . . the true meaning (of Christmas) is everybody together and happy."

"I don't know nothing worse than being too poor to give something. It aches your heart."

"Christmas is a blue day in jail."

"I know I couldn't go see my family and say Merry Christmas. I know I'd get throwed out."

"Never nobody loved me. I have been lonely all my life."

You will catch glimpses of the "old" Christmas in this book, a hint here and there that Christmas is still sturdy, no matter how battered, and you may be reminded, too, that the word "holiday" comes from the two words, "holy day." Christmas, these people seem to be saying, may take a great deal more abuse before it succumbs, although there is no assurance that it will survive in warm and genuine form.

Unless there is some restraint in the compulsive celebration of a thoughtless Christmas this season as a time of peace and goodwill may indeed be doomed.

Until then, however, there is solace in the fact that there survives even in the most unlikely places the shining and selfless concept of Christmas as a time to give rather than to get.

Basically, that is what the persons quoted in these pages are saying: That Christmas is love or it is nothing. That Christmas is, indeed, "everybody together and happy."

ROBERT CROMIE

Introduction

"Christmas . . . where's it at?"

This was the question we asked the people in this book—prisoners, the destitute, the lonely, the aged, kids, men in flophouses, young people who have been taking drugs, residents of a half-way house, and a man in the lounge of a skin flick movie on Christmas Eve.

"We'll protect your anonymity," was our pledge to all we interviewed. We promised not to give people's names, and to avoid "summarizing" them in short introductory paragraphs to their comments.

"We'll respect your dignity" was our commitment to them. It meant simply, we would not comment on what the people said, so as to promote our own point of view. Anything less, we felt, would be using them as persons.

We, therefore, have not authored this book. We have listened to the people and then reported their words.

Our report is not a long sad tale of woe, but rather a human tapestry woven by people willing to share personal thoughts and experiences about the most emotion-packed of all holidays.

Our purpose was not to say what Christmas is or how it could or should be, but rather to present the tapestry to the world, much as a scientist would present a find or a historian reveal a significant document.

Both of us whose names appear on this book have worked in promoting "The Neediest Children's Christmas Fund." In order to do this, we had to write about the poor at Christmastime and encourage others to do so. We both came to a point where we felt compelled instead to let the poor and the disenfranchised express themselves about Christmas.

It was not without strong feeling or emotion, however, that the two of us turned reporter in this instance. It's one thing to build up to Christmas by seeing the decorations in the department store windows and yet another to see the ornaments and trees in the bare rooms of the destitute or on the bars of the tiers in the women's section of the county jail.

We particularly thank our wives for helping us get on with the work.

We have also sprinkled here and there a few jarring thoughts about Christmas. The authors of these comments run the gamut from Tiny Tim (the original one) to Playboy magazine. They are not meant as an orientation, but they do offer insights into how and why Christmas is put together in this country and time.

The title of the book, "The Death of Christmas" may be understood in a number of ways. It is a question for some; a statement of fact for others; a profound (if true) theological observation and rebuttal argument for those who would and do keep to the spirit of December 25.

For those chronically and disproportionately left out of it, the title may be a wish or even a prayer for the death of Christmas.

For many the situation is clearly ambiguous as they seem to be saying, "Christmas is dead. Long live Christmas."

Acknowledgment

Several years ago, there was much talk of "The Death of God." As critics have often noted since, that movement is long since dead, but God is still going strong.

To be fair, it should be said that the young theologians who first postulated the philosophy did not mean that God himself was dead, but that, to too many in our increasingly secularized society, he might as well be.

So it is with "The Death of Christmas." Christmas is not dead. Part of its recurring miracle is that in each holiday season there comes a moment for most of us when we are suddenly caught up once again in its true spirit, when we realize anew how much more blessed it is to give than to receive. The relentless commercialization and vulgarization that threaten to reduce all our holidays simply to selling seasons, may make that moment of Christmas insight come later each year. But come it does.

However, if Christmas is not dead, it might as well

be for too many of the unfortunate, the hungry, the displaced and the lonely. The vignettes in this book tell the story of 43 such people. Its purpose is not to mark the death of Christmas, but—through the contributions of those who purchase a copy—to help bring Christmas to many children who might not otherwise be able to enjoy it.

All proceeds will go to the Neediest Children's Christmas Fund, which was conceived by the hard working Mrs. Elizabeth Watkins of the Cook County Department of Public Aid. She collected money through the Fund so that mothers could put a hot holiday meal on the table, or buy their children a pair of warm mittens, or earmuffs or perhaps a toy.

But because funds were pitifully limited, they could help only the very neediest of the needy. In 1969, for example, they collected $22,000, which allowed them to give $5 checks to the mothers of 4,400 out of 197,000 needy youngsters.

In 1970, however, the Fund received extraordinary help from the media—among many others, from Paul Molloy of the *Chicago Sun-Times,* himself the father of eight; Wally Phillips of WGN-Radio; Bob Cromie of the *Chicago Tribune;* John Fischetti, editorial page cartoonist of the *Chicago Daily News;* and Commodore, cartoonist for the *Chicago Defender.* As a result, we raised $140,000 last year, and so were able to help mothers give a present to 28,000 of 250,000 needy younsters. That was a six-fold increase, and we hope to do even better in the future.

Our eventual goal: a present for every needy child in Chicago.

Proceeds of this book will help. It is being published as a public service by Follett Publishing Company. The authors have waived all royalties.

If, after reading these stories, you want to help bring Christmas back to life for additional children, a tax deductible contribution can be sent to:

> Neediest Children's Christmas Fund
> Cook County Department of Public Aid
> 318 West Adams Street
> Chicago, Illinois 60606

The kids and their mothers will be grateful.

NORMAN ROSS
Chairman, Neediest
Children's Christmas
Fund
DAVID L. DANIEL
Director, Cook County
Department of Public
Aid

Contents

"I Woke up this Morning with the Glory

the death of Christmas

"You Want to Listen to My Story?"

It is Christmas Eve. We both here to have drink in this bar. I tell you a Christmas story you not believe. You want to listen?

"My mother lives in Puerto Rico. Before I born, she make the 'promisa.' That is like the oath. She promise to Virgin if she get her wish granted, she name the next baby after her or after her Son. My mother get her wish. Then I born. She call me Jesus Maria for good measure.

"Always, though, I not be satisfied with life. I try to kill myself, even in high school. I study encyclopedia of poisons. First, I try aspirins and get sick like you never see. Later, I try sleeping pills and I sleep for two days and two nights and they not think I live. Finally, I tried Veronal. But I started praying and I threw the pills under the bed.

"You still want to hear my story?

"I tried drinking myself to death by becoming a drunkard.

"Never nobody loves me. I been lonely all my life."

"One time, I get drunk and I put my head down on the railroad track and I pass out. I wake up in police

1

station. A woman she see me and she call police.

"I am now 55 years old and I am ready to wait for death. I feel someone looks after me. I feel it is God and He not let me kill myself. It is maybe because of the 'promisa' and because I have His name.

"I'm glad you listen to my story. Maybe, you not see this is Christmas story. I do. My name is Jesus."

"... an indigenous, national Christmas developed in this country during the nineteenth century which differed from prior celebrations in the British Isles and in several European nations. It crystalized in most parts of the United States by 1860 and altered little in essentials after that time. Commercial influences entered the festival during the latter part of the last century, but made their strongest impact on it after 1920. Secular aspects of the celebration now rival the Christian observances of the occasion, and would probably persist even if its religious significance should diminish. It is also clear that the bonds of family, brotherhood, and even nationalism have become intertwined with the symbolism of the celebration, and few people are immune to such a combination of influences."—James H. Barnett, "The American Christmas" 1954

"Last Year, I Had $7 to Buy Christmas With."

Last year, I had $7 to buy Christmas with. That didn't include any money to buy a tree. I bought my daughter a pair of mittens. The little ones, I got each a truck from the dimestore. The two big ones got 79¢ rockets that you can shoot up into the air. I was able to buy a little candy and some nuts. That was it. The $1.50 I had left bought a chicken.

"My children never get birthday gifts. Then, here comes all these commercials starting in September. They never tell the children how much things cost. The kids think they give them away. I'm sad from when they start to advertise until Christmas is over.

"The hardest part in my house is that we were not always on welfare. When I was married, the kids had anything they wanted. Now, when the kids ask, you

4

tell them you'll try, but you know you can't buy it for them.

"We went from an income of $800 a month to one of less than $300. It was like going from your house to the streets.

"I hate Christmas now. I grew up poor and I vowed that my kids would have what I didn't.

"I wonder how many people ever had to get up on Christmas morning and face their kids and not have anything to give them? It's really bad on welfare.

"You try to save—everybody does that—but an emergency always comes up. Then it means food off your table or clothes off their backs.

"How do you explain to kids that you can't buy them nothing, expecially when they see other kids with bikes or trikes and, when they get older, radios and even a television.

"My oldest boy is emotionally disturbed, and he wants a poodle for Christmas. He found one and I told him he could keep it if no one claimed it, but the owner was found after two days. He knows only one thing: he wants a poodle. The psychiatrist asked him what's his hobby and my son told him, 'Dogs.' But there's no room in my budget for his poodle.

"We can't even afford the $5 for a Christmas tree. If you spend the money on a tree, you can't buy gifts. And Christmas is not Christmas without a tree. Last year, my kids found a tree in an alley that someone had for a Christmas party and had thrown out. They dragged it home and were really happy. Maybe, some generous person could find a way to donate trees to the poor on Christmas.

"I can't explain Christmas to my kids. I'm unhappy and my kids know it. When you have little or nothing for a child at Christmas, you say something spontaneous that'll hit his mind, you hope.

"At the second, I think the child hates you. He thinks you really don't want to give him something.

"As a mother, you always fear that the child is going to grow up and later say to you, 'You never gave anything to me, why should I care for you.' Every poor mother fears this in her heart.

"We don't want to be on welfare. I have worked and I would like to be out working now. But I have an emotionally disturbed son, 12. I was told by the psychiatrist that I had to be home when he came home after school and if he came home for lunch so that he would feel wanted and secure when he returns home from school. I can work. I'm not sick, my son is.

"Maybe, if people would just admit there were such reasons for people being on welfare, things would be different.

"I'd like a new coat for Christmas, but by the time you buy for the kids, there's nothing left. I got the coat I'm wearing out of a garbage can. It buttons with a safety pin, but it'd be warm if it just had lining in the sleeves.

"You try to save. We get $281 a month. And $4.50 of that is for laundry. Well, it costs me $5 a week for laundry, so there's over $15 a month lost out of your budget.

"My problems, however, seem so small in comparison with other families with whom I've come into contact. Somebody recently gave me a donation of mittens. I gave some of them to a Latin family with 9 kids. The father has TB and the little baby, pneumonia. My, you'd think I had given them a million dollars. I wish I had had a camera to take pictures of their smiles.

"A woman I grew up with last Christmas had only a pot of pinto beans and 12 tortillas for Christmas, and I gave her the pot of pinto beans. She told her kids that Santa had run out of toys before he reached their house. The kids accepted it, because they never had very much anyway. Then they finally had a Christmas about a month later because an organization heard about the family and gave the kids some toys. They never did quite understand why their Christmas was a month later than everybody else's.

"This year, I have been trying to help at Hull House and collect toys for families around here for Christmas. We have contacted 30 families so far. They have, on the average, 6 kids each. We've found they're not even looking for Christmas.

"We're going to have a Christmas party for a total of about 350 kids. Many of the toys we've collected so far are broken. Even with my little ones that's all right, it doesn't make much difference because they'll be broken right away anyway.

"We've begged the biggest department stores for some toys, but they say, 'We simply don't have anything in our budget this year for such donations.'

So we've decided to ask all the stores in the Lincoln—Belmont area each for one toy. So far, we've been kinda sucessful, but we're going to go back and try again."

"Annually, Americans spend more than $10 billion on Christmas gifts, an average of about $5 per gift."—News Item

"I'm Not Going to Stand on My Head and Spit Quarters for Christmas."

I'm not going to stand on my head and spit quarters for Christmas. I believe in Christmas, but not in all that bullshit about Santa Claus.

"I got an aunt who really got the spirit of Christmas. She sends a sheet of notebook paper and writes on it, 'Merry Christmas. Love, Aunt Mattie.' "

10

"Christmas Is for the Rich to Enjoy, the Middle Class to Imitate and the Poor to Watch."

On Christmas, two years ago, nobody was up in the house but me and my two friends. I was in a big paranoid bag. We were dropping acid.

"Two days before Christmas we went out along Lake Shore Drive and ripped off the lights from a tree and snatched a tree off someone's front porch. We leaned the tree up in the apartment because we had no stand. We had the tree and lights for a long time.

"I was living with a girl at the time and it was about then that I freaked out.

"We took in the tree mostly out of tradition and for

11

something to do. Christmas doesn't mean anything too special.

"There's too much expected of people on Christmas. There's just too many roles people have to live up to. You have to be filled up so much with Christmas cheer. You're supposed to forget everything that's happening.

"You're supposed to say, 'So what if there's people being killed in Viet Nam, "Merry Christmas." '

"Even the fact that the only people able to celebrate Christmas are people who have enough money to pay tribute to almighty consumer economy is something you're supposed to ignore.

"I think Christmas around Chicago is one of the most pitiful times of the year because you see how bad things are.

"Everybody's on his own little trip saying and seeing how nice things are while it's actually the time people are most pushed around.

"Christmas is for the rich to enjoy, the middle class to imitate, and the poor to watch.

"Last Christmas and this one had some meaning for us. A group of young people who are with Hull House and who all had been on speed or drugs got a couple of turkeys and invited all the kids they knew without homes and had a feast. We panhandled the money for the food. It was great. There were 9 kids altogether."

"I Was Really Thinking of Going Home for Christmas, But... I Would Have Ruined Their Christmas by Showing up."

When you've faced Christmas alone, your whole idea of it changes.

"Christmas on the South Side or a lot of places in Chicago is a lot different from Christmas in the suburbs.

"I've been on drugs, but now I'm making it. I was really thinking of going home for Christmas, but when I thought how my appearance and my views have changed—how different I was—I would have ruined their Christmas by showing up. To them, it would have been like inviting a bum off the street. They would have thrown me out. They cannot accept me for myself, the way I am now.

"It was the Christmas that I was 15 when I learned the difference. I had always gone along with a happy view of the occasion. That year I bought a lot of gifts. My Mom told me all the gifts I had bought were wrong. I told her they were supposed to be gifts from me to the family, not from her. She slapped me and sent me to my room. I had bought my little brother a toy and she told me I should have bought him a jumpsuit. It changed my whole view.

"My fondest memory is still the smile on my little brother's face when he got a gigantic candy cane. The true meaning is everybody together and happy and that's what I'd like to see. In that sense, I'd think Christmas is the best idea in the world."

"As a Religious Festival, Christmas Is Very Much Dead. As a Capitalist Ceremony, It Is Alive."

The Church isn't keeping Christmas alive anymore. It's the capitalists who are.

"The Church doesn't have the people anymore. It's not keeping them together.

"It's the capitalists. They're the ones who promote Christmas. They say, 'Buy this . . . because it's expected of you.' You're supposed to give the best—like if you don't, you're not giving anything.

"That's their whole advertising angle. I have to give this to so and so. I'm supposed to spend as much

16

as I can.

"The thing that ruins Christmas is that you are not free to give or do what you want. You're doing things because they're expected of you, not because you want to. You're doing things not to make people happy, but to impress people.

"The other side is: How much did I get and all this garbage. You're not really thinking.

"I'm 22 years old and my family's middle class so I have to go home for Christmas. I'd just as well prefer to be with friends.

"I don't have very much money and neither does my brother and his wife. Yet, we all have to give gifts to people we see 3 times a year. My mother suggested we just have a dinner and forget about the gifts. But the others argued that it's breaking tradition.

"As a religious festival, Christmas is very much dead. As a capitalist ceremony, it is alive."

"An extra shopping day proved a Christmas bonus for the nation's retailers last week, enabling most to equal or move slightly ahead of last year's holiday business.

"Stores backed up the additional day with longer selling hours and heavier promotion in a determined effort to bring their figures up.

"Heaviest concentration was in rtw [ready-to-wear] and accessories, with furs and jewelry showing late spurts."—Women's Wear Daily Dec. 28, 1970

"We Are All Children at Christmastime. I Need Clothes. I Need Panties."

I got about 24 kids on this block who won't have no Christmas. I could give it to them if I had it. I don't have it.

"When I used to work, I used to help people paying rent and buying them clothes and getting kids presents. I just loves to give things.

"I don't know nothing worse than being too poor to give something. It aches your heart. I just feels like a dog.

"The little kids next door. I used to Santa Claus them. Now, I can't do no Santa Clausing. I can't give them nothing.

"Seven years ago, someone bought me a little silver Christmas tree. It don't got any lights on it or balls or anything.

"Last year, I had such a bad Christmas I didn't put it up. I was so disgusted.

"Christmas was always wonderful to me till the last few years. For poor people and people used to having things and haven't got them, Christmas is miserable.

"Most everything I got, I gets from second-hand stores. I haven't had no new clothes since 1961. Right now, I don't have one piece of underwear. Not a slip. Not a pair of panties. I wears size 52 and you don't get things size 52 second-hand at the Salvation Army.

"Still, I'm glad God has been as good to me as He has. People ask me if I gonna make it. I think I has made it. I'm 65 years old and I'm filled with the Holy Ghost.

"Christmas is the birth of Christ and it is best we accept that.

"When you exchange gifts, there is no blessing in that. It is no good. I never gives anything to anybody who didn't need it.

"I been in the market and I seen an old man or an old woman order two pork chops and then tell them to take one back when they saw how much it cost. When I had money, I told the butcher to give them 6 pork chops and I pay.

"You look at the children in this neighborhood. You look at any one child and you see he not have enough of the right thing. You can look at them and see they not get enough cod liver oil. They not get enough orange juice or milk or anything.

"People with money should endeavor to put out a little more money to help people out.

"We are all children at Christmas time. I need clothes. I need panties. I like to be able pay some of my bills. I'd like to get something good to eat.

"My lights were off for 5 weeks and they just turn them back on a week ago. Now, they threaten to turn my gas off.

"I think my social worker is a Nazi and hates colored people. There are several older men staying here. I think welfare out to help them out more. They're bums to some people, but they're not gangsters. They don't belong to no Panthers. One is 87 years old. They're all good people. They're all Democrats.

"This is something people don't know. As a rule, people on welfare, they don't get their check during Christmastime. And Christmas is like death, a nightmare for those that don't get nothing."

"AT LEAST CHRISTMAS SHOULD BE EQUAL

But it isn't.

By now, most kids have forgotten the gifts they got last year. Unless they didn't get any. There are a lot of wrongs in this world that still aren't right. But Christmas seems like a good time to start righting them. Because nothing seems so wrong as a child facing Christmas with an empty stocking. Or an empty stomach. Especially when there's something we can do."—Radio station WVON Solicitation for poor kids

"A Man Shouldn't Have to Suffer This Kind of Loneliness."

I didn't expect to see this many men here on Christmas Eve. A man shouldn't have to suffer this kind of loneliness.

"More families celebrate holidays than bachelors do. To us, it's just another day and we get tired of our lonely looking room, whether it's a holiday or not.

"I'm tired of going to bars and sitting there, a pigeon all alone. At this kind of movie, I get a little solitude and I'm able to console myself without just being a prospect for a prostitute—something a man's not always able to financially have anyway.

"There's a similarity between the kid who can't have any toys for Christmas and the man who can't have the sexual companionship he wants. I can sympathize with the boy, because I too am not

24

disposed to have what I want. The desire for a toy in a little boy is an early substitute, I think, for his original concern for sexual companionship.

"Christmas offers so much of a response to childish ambition. It shows that grown-ups are looking down into his childish world and it helps keep a view of the future in mind.

"The presents show something done in the child's behalf and offers him a promising future to look forward to. In the early stages of life, you have to have something to look forward to, if only a piece of candy.

"The main thing a child remembers through the years is Christmas.

"Now, at my age, I find myself neutral to Christmas, but I'm sort of open-minded like I am to nudity. I find myself constantly observing to come to some sort of conclusion about it."

"If You Got Somebody That Cares and Who Loves Ya, I Guess Christmas Is a Pretty Good Thing."

If you got somebody that cares and who loves ya, I guess Christmas is a pretty good thing. Otherwise, if yer alone, it's pretty depressing.

"If you have something to share, that puts the whole spirit into the thing. You take myself or some guy alone in a hotel or a bar like myself, what does he have to share?

"My Christmases have been pretty good. I've always given something. Not this Christmas. I've a retarded brother at a state school. I've had to write him that there was nowhere to come.

"I'm down. I used to have an apartment and money

in my pocket to take him to a show. Not this year. I couldn't have him come to see me when I havn't got anything.

"I've always had a pretty good Christmas. This one's going to be melancholy."

"And how did Tiny Tim behave?" asked Mrs. Cratchit.

"As good as gold," said Bob, "And better. Somehow, he gets thoughtful, sitting by himself so much, and thinks the strangest thoughts you ever heard. He told me, coming home, that he hoped the people saw him in the church, because he was a cripple, and it might be pleasant to them to remember, upon Christmas day, who it was who made lame beggars walk and blind men see."— Charles Dickens, *A Christmas Carol*

"Take Away This Dark Cloud That Is Over Us and Our Families on This Day."

To some guys, Christmas is a very foul moment. To me, it's a blackout. We were all reared up with the idea that Christmas is something bright, special, and good. Well, then give some of us guys in jail here a chance. Give us bonds and eliminate long court dates. Take away this dark cloud that is over us and our families on this day."

"An Organization Comes Into Jails and They Line You up Against the Wall Like Cattle to Get a Bag of Candy."

An organization comes into here at Christmas time and they line you up against the wall like cattle to get a bag of candy. It's charity. They tell you, in effect, that if you don't behave and don't line up like good cattle, you don't get a bag.

"It takes a lot out of you. You feel they're prejudging you and seem to be thinking, 'I'm not going to take any bullshit from you fellows. I know how you are.'

"They—and other organizations pull the same

31

thing—don't present it to the guys like you do to a normal group of guys and say, 'Look, fellows, we only got so much candy to give out here in the jail so we're going to need your cooperation.'

"Of course, the men here'll steal, but it won't happen if they present themselves right. One or two would grab, but they can't out-argue or dare to antogonize the other 60 guys here. They know they couldn't get away with it.

"I'm not saying that these organizations ought not to come in here and give out presents and new suits, but I don't think they ought to prejudge these fellows for the price of a little candy. It's the attitude that has to be changed.

"This prejudging is what is at the root of a lot of the problems around here. The judges first of all have to stop doing it and every time they see a man with record of being in jail, say, 'Well, here comes another one of those cases.'

"You really see it when you come through the lock-up. I'm not hung up on the black-white thing, but, man! Say 10 men come through the lock-up and 5 are white and 5 black. Usually about 3 of them are let out on recognizance bond at the discretion of the judge. Usually all 3 are white or at least the majority are. In the majority of cases, black men are simply not given recognizance bonds.

"It's Christmas and these fellows could be out, but they're not. It's little wonder Christmas doesn't have the same importance for the poor man it used to. It doesn't have that same feeling.

"I spent last Christmas and the one before that in the state prison. This time I've been in three months 'on the suspicion of the possession of heroin' and I use those words carefully.

"One of these days, they should try to get down to the root of the problem. If a guy is back 3 or 4 times, rather than say he is a hardened criminal, they should say incarceration is just not working."

"There were 5,324 inmates in Illinois jails last March 15, according to a new federal report, and of those, only 1,816—or 34 per cent were convicted and serving sentences. The rest—66 per cent were awaiting trial and arraignment."—News Item

"A Few of Us Are Gonna Try to Get Together and Give a Singing, a Telling Joke Show, on Christmas Morning."

Christmas doesn't appeal to me. The simple reason is I'm locked up.

"You can't talk as loud as you'd like. You can't sing. You'd think they'd let us have some kind of recreation. You can't go in your cell during the day. You'd think they'd let you enjoy yourself some during the day. They don't even let us congregate.

"To me, when I was small, Christmas was something nice. Now, things have changed a lot.

"When you're little, you expect presents. I'm not

getting nothing.

"I've been in jail most of my life. It's a lot different than out on the streets. When I was free, I had the Christmas spirit. I'd get out and buy presents for my friends and relatives. Now, I don't think about anybody but myself.

"They try to make it better for you. Maybe, we'll get better food and Operation Breadbasket will distribute candy and underwear and T-shirts, but it ain't just right.

"No matter what, I don't have much to give. Somebody gives me a candybar, but I don't have one to give. All you have to offer to the guy next to you around here is your friendship.

"A few of us are gonna try to get together and give a singing and telling jokes show on Christmas morning.

"My first Christmas in jail, I thought it'd be just like on the streets. I thought we'd get some presents and have candy and apples and oranges. A few fellows sang some songs and that was it.

"My mother and father died when I was 15 and I've been in and out jail ever since then. This time I'm in on a charge of murder.

"No, I'd have to say that up here behind it, Christmas just doesn't mean that much to me."

"I've Given up Religion. I Don't Seem to Have Any Luck, in Religion or Anywhere."

Christmas is a blue day in jail. I know. I have been in prison for the last 30 years or more. The last one with my family was in 1937. I remember I got a wooden train and a sled.

"My folks died of TB and I was put in a foster home. Since then I have spent almost all of my time in either detention homes or jails. It's been small stuff, mainly stealing.

"Things just don't look too damn good. First time I've been in jail for something I'm innocent of. What I am supposed to be guilty of is the attempted murder of two policemen.

"I don't know. You'd think just before Christmas, they'd pry into some cases. A lot of them are not guilty or are just the victims of society. I don't mean me so much. I mean especially the younger men. Maybe, it's just one out of 10, but they should do it and give them a chance to be home with their families.

"Christmas is a nice idea with the presents and all that, but I've given up religion. I just don't seem to have any luck, in religion or anywhere."

"Christmas Is
Just Another Day."

When you're in jail, Christmas is just another day. You don't look forward to it. The only day you look forward to is the day you'll get out.

"We'll have rolled turkey for lunch with all the trimmings. The Salvation Army, I understand, used to give a bag of candy or something. Not anymore.

"The only ones talk about Christmas around here are the ones hope to be home for it."

"Christmas in My Life Is Very Personal to Me."

This is not like truth what I'm in here for (homocide). It just seems like mostly a dream.

"Last year it was beautiful. We all had a reunion at the church—that's where the reunion begins—Sunday morning at the church and then we'd all go out for breakfast.

"This is the first time I've been away from them. My wife's working, living off of our savings account. We have two youngsters 10 and 14. It's just like a dream not being with my family for breakfast like this.

"Christmas in my life is very personal to me. I use it to myself, not like a holiday but like the symbol of the birth of Christ. I use Christmas as a meaning. It's like a dream not being with them."

"There's a Lot of Ornaments Here in the Women's Tiers, but the Christmas Spirit Doesn't Extend Into Here."

There's a lot of ornaments here in the women's tiers, but the Christmas spirit doesn't really extend into here. People have too many problems on their minds.

"Christmas morning was the time I was arrested last year. I have two little boys, 6 and 3 years old. I haven't seen them in the 12 months since then.

"I have been in contact with my family, but I really miss them. This is a sad and depressing place to be on Christmas."

"It Doesn't Matter Where You Are, Christmas Is the Rebirth of Christ."

Christmas here in jail? To me, Christmas is the rebirth of Christ and it doesn't matter where you are, your attitude should be the same.

"Me, though, I'm worried to death. I try not to think, not to think about things. You try to pull them back as much as you can till you're alone and then you can't help but think about them."

"If I Had the Money, I'd Be Out on Bond for Christmas."

Christmas is just another day to me. I'm in jail. I'm not happy about it. It's just Christmas, that's all. If I had the money, I'd be out on bond for it."

44

"Over 50 cities (outside of Illinois) . . . have found that poor people released on their own recognizance will show up in court more frequently than people released on money bail."—Joseph R. Rowan Executive Director, The John Howard Association

"I'm an Old Woman and I Never Been Near a Jail Before."

I'm 51 years old and this is the worst Christmas I ever had or dreamed of. I'm an old woman and I never been near a jail before.

"I'm used to a Christmas when you get all the kids together and the grandchildren and you put up the tree.

"Worst of all I'm in here for something I know nothing about. My brother got beat up and I had been to his apartment to wait for his wife who was missing, so I got accused of it.

"Oh, this is the worst Christmas I ever had in all my 51 years.

"I just hope someone in my family will make a Christmas for mother. She's 88 years old and I'm the only one to look out for her. Oh, I do hope they take care of her.

"Other than that, I do know that I'm thankful to be alive and I know some folks got it even worse."

"Christmas in America Is 5 Minutes."

Christmas is a plastic and a false bombardment of the senses. You are stunned by the colors and by the new gadgets. Out of all of this is supposed to come this Christian feeling of giving.

"It's coercion. Some people have got their ship together to make money. I can't relate to that kind of giving.

"Christmas in America is 5 minutes of self-indulged joy of giving presents to someone.

"I object to that Christmas totally. It is not a rebirth of anything. It is not a rebirth of emotions or feelings that are genuine.

"What kind of a sense of giving is there on the expressways at rush hour? What kind of a sense of giving can it be when Christmas is messing up so many lives elsewhere?

"To top it off, the profits go back into the stock-holders' pockets. The investment is not returned to the people. In a sense, the money going into Christmas is going into a increase merely in profits.

"Let's face it. They have the perfect formula for making money. Throw in tradition, toss in Christianity, and the media puts the coercion into it.

"The Christian ideal of giving oneself is changed into buying toy guns.

"It is TV, not Christianity, telling me what my child and I should have and do for Christmas.

"The Church doesn't give a shit about Christmas. The Church basically is also telling you, 'Buy, buy, buy to give.'

"The most 'right on' Christmas I ever celebrated was the 'Black Christmas' we had in Milwaukee in 1968. The Black people led by Fr. Groppi were encouraged not to celebrate Christmas at all except to march on Christmas night. And they didn't celebrate, they boycotted all the merchants who were discriminating against the Blacks while profiteering off of them. Man, that was the most meaningful and significant Christmas I'll ever spend.

"Christmas is valueless. What can people really give? I can only give of myself, but the media coerce our supposedly good intentions into a phony reality of what giving is.

"I'm going to celebrate Christmas and give the most meaningful gifts I can to members of my family. It'll be poetry for my father, a book on a radical priest for my mother, maybe something made

49

of leather in a 'Freak' culture store for my sister. But the only reason I'm even doing that is that I have a sense of responsibility, that I should share what my parents are into.

"The fact is there isn't going to be any Christmas in America for a long, long time. Not until we look past the 5 minutes of self-endulged joy from giving presents to the 5 minutes of life left for some child in Africa, Viet Nam, or Jordan."

"Baby Jesus Wants Us to Celebrate."

Christmas is presents, a Christmas tree, decorating, ornaments, and going to see Santa Claus and wrapping up those presents and that's all.

"Baby Jesus wants us to celebrate Christmas—that's why we do it."

"Christmas Is Life to the Kids."

O ther folks what is poor, they do the same I do, they makes the most of Christmas.

"This year is something, though. I has lung cancer and I needs an operation. I'se not going into the hospital till after Christmas, cus if I should not live through this one, I wants to be with my kids for Christmas.

"This make it four years. When things got really tough, my husband cut out. I got 8 kids under 12. I decided to stick it out as long as I could and take care of myself.

"Last year, I feel like giving up. I almost did.

"It's hard raising 8 kids by yourself. The welfare, they's the only ones that help, and they don't give ya nuff.

"If I should die from this operation, my kids are gonna get it. Other people, they can't handle my kids the way I can. It ain't easy keeping them out of gangs and seeing that they gets back and forth to school safe.

"The headaches comes when yer my age. Before I got married, I was gonna see the world. I shoulda done that and never got myself tied down.

"I been saving up for three weeks. I gonna get a aluminum tree at the drugstore for $10. Ya can get one cheeper if ya shops around, but I can't do much going accounta I's sick.

"Christmas is life to the kids—waking up to find out a little something and that tree.

"Last Christmas, the Urban Progress center gave us toys for the kids. Most of the stuff was things run by batteries, like a truck and a telephone. Myself, I didn't get nothing. A poor person ain't got a prayer unless someone help us.

"My brother and his wife, they is as poor as I is. They don't have nothing for Christmas.

"Two years ago, I didn't have any money to buy them toys. I told them Santa Claus maybe come up next year. I said maybe I have some money then and I can pay him and he bring some toys.

"This year, I use the rent money for January and then I pay that month's rent next month in order to give them some toys. I already told them they'd have to wait till after Christmas to get any toys.

"I don't know what I's gonna do yet. The little money I does has for Christmas I should buy them overshoes. I has 7 in school and they only got tennis shoes to wear.

"But Christmas and Halloween, that's the two big days for the kids, but it ain't gonna be nothing if they don't get any toys. I feel hurt I can't buy them nothing, but I don't show it to them.

"After Christmas, the teachers over there to school, they lets the kids bring over their toys to show them. My kids, they ain't gonna have any till maybe January.

"And me, I'd love a good old warm jacket for the winter. The jacket I's has, it's raggedy.

"Being poor is a rough way to go. I says give me my flowers now while I can enjoy them."

"There are five or six important guides which, I believe, would continue and preserve Christmas as a festival of hope. They do not guarantee it.

"The first is that the tree should be real . . ."
Eugene McCarthy McCall's, Dec. 1970

"Christmas. . .Do Not Have the Same Importance It Used to."

Christmas is only a symbol far as the poor man is concerned. It do not have the same importance it used to. It do not have that same feeling.

"If you have money and a chance to spend it, it go mainly for food and bare necessities. If anything left over, you start thinking of toys maybe.

"You have to develop this attitude, even though it's bad."

"Christmas Is Nothing Really Special to Me. My Life Just Goes on Day After Day, the Same Thing."

I wake up people in a half-way house. That's for people who have been in mental hospitals. Fortunately, it's one of the few good hotels like this. I'll say this for Christmas. The people even greet me a little better at Christmas when I knock on their doors to wake them up in the mornings.

"Christmas, however, is nothing really special to me. My life just goes on day after day, the same thing.

"I spent 20 years as an investigator for the state department of labor. One day, I was beaten and

58

robbed and suffered a loss of memory. That's why I'm here.

"I'm divorced and have three grown sons, but they don't contact me. I'm pretty much resigned to the fact they are grown up.

"When my sons were small, we really looked forward to Christmas. First there were tricycles and then bikes.

"I have two grandchildren, I think. I don't believe my oldest son is married.

"For most people, Christmas is a very joyous season."

"At the State Hospital, We Got a Nice Meal for Christmas."

I always thought people were supposed to enjoy themselves at Christmas because it is a special day of the year.

"TV's kinda nice at Christmas with its special programs they have sometimes.

"Then, sometimes, I get a present—a dress or perfume from my family.

"I always thought everybody enjoyed themselves at Christmas. I like the Christmas tree and downtown is nicely decorated. At the state hospital, we got a nice meal for Christmas.

"Everybody seems happy around Christmas."

"After Christmas I'm Broke, Really Broke, for a Long While, That's Why It Hurts."

I spent several Christmases in a state mental hospital. The first two were in 'hydro,' the worst ward in the place. The first Christmas they had me in restraints. The second I spent getting shots in my butt. I will tell you this—I fought everyone of those shots. I slapped them in the mouth.

"I especially enjoy Christmas now, because I get an opportunity to entertain people not as well off as I.

"I save up real hard—I'm on public aid—so I can entertain for Christmas. But afterwards I'm broke, really broke for a long while, that's why it hurts.

"Mentally, Christmas can get the poor and lonely out of the rut. I love it.

"As far as spending any of it with my family.

61

Bah—humbug. After I got out of the hospital, my family wanted to be real good to me. But, when I was in, they didn't give a damn.

"I have a foster aunt who is old. She's the one who makes Christmas worthwhile for me. She always cared when my family didn't. She appreciates any little thing you give her, no matter how small it is."

"Being at Home. To Me That's Christmas."

I'd look forward to Christmas if I could get any part of it.

"I need clothes. I can't go outside if I don't have enough clothes. I could use a shawl and boots. I call them 'hard clothes.' That's what I need.

"I'd like to get lots of presents. Anything I didn't care about, I could find people who could use it.

"Being at home. To me that's Christmas. But I'm not at home."

"Christmas Is All Right."

My landlady's trying to put me out because I gave my children a Christmas and I only paid her part of the rent at this time.

"Her only other gripe is that I got behind one time on my rent because the welfare check was late. She was real mad that I bought my children some Christmas.

"I don't understand. I told her everyone else pays by the week. She lives in Skokie.

"The landlady told me two days before Christmas that I had one week to move.

"I have 4 rooms and the roaches are so bad. I spray and spray and I can't get rid of them.

"I pay her $150 a month rent. Something like $125 is alloted by welfare, and the rest I pay out of my food and clothes money. Still, she brought me soap and paint and wanted me to wash down the walls and to paint them.

"My sister and I both had a chance to go to a Christmas party and get some presents for the kids, but she's on general assistance and I'm on A.D.C. so she doesn't get as much as me so I stayed home and babysat for both our kids so she could go.

"I told my children they'd only get one or two things for Christmas and they understood pretty good. The children don't get the things they want from seeing television, but that's the way it is.

"We didn't have a Christmas last year. I was working then. My daughter got sick just before Christmas and was in the hospital for a week. I missed a week's work and none of my four children got a single gift.

"This year, people gave us a tree, and welfare money is providing our food or we would not have a Christmas.

"I wish people who don't have much would get something and people in jail would be let out for Christmas so they can get food for their families.

"Christmas is all right, but I've talked to several people and they say, 'I wish Christmas would never come or that it would be over.'"

"Christmas Is a Racket."

Christmas is a racket. It's all right for kids that don't know any better."

A very old, poor, and Black man, Christmas Day

"I Woke Up This Morning with the Glory of the Lord Shining Around Me."

Today is the day every man ought to appreciate. A Man gave His life to try to save men—that was our Lord Jesus Christ. I woke up this morning with all the glory of the Lord shining around me."

"I Wish for Better Holidays [Chanukahs]."

There is no Christmas for me. My Christmas is a Jewish holiday, Chanukah. But my people are all dead and there is no place to go for Chanukah.

"I celebrate it right here. I've been sick and it's hard for me to go anywhere.

"When your family is dead, you don't celebrate it except in the synagogue. I light up candles for them.

"I'm 68 years old. I never had a family of my own. I had a married brother and his wife, but they both passed away.

"It takes money to go. If I had money, I could go somewhere for the holidays, but I don't. I live off of society. I get $55.35 a month from Social Security. The Jewish boys who go to the Russian bath, they help me out too.

"I've had a lot of accidents and everything. I make the most of it by myself. I wish for better holidays."

"A midi coat is a must if you want your dog to be fashionably attired for a Christmas morning walk. Particularly stylish are the ones with the new 'wet' look. For a touch of comfort plus fashion, select a coat lined with fake fur. Complete the outfit with matching hat and boots. Rubber or plastic, boots protect paws from salt and chemicles on snowy streets." —Dog and Cat Column, *Chicago Tribune*

"I Ain't Got No Christmas."

I ain't got no Christmas. I was with the Salvation Army. I was driving a truck, but I got throwed out three days before Christmas.

"If I woulda stuck it out, I'd had a good Christmas dinner and everything. I got throwed out cuz I came in a little tight.

"Ya hear that record on the radio. It's like the fella's singing, 'Christmas is the most wonderful time of the year.' . . . well, yah, like he says, 'When your loved ones are near.'

"I know I couldn't go see my family and say, 'Merry Christmas.' I know I'd get throwed out. I'm more or less an outcast.

"I got a niece I kinda raised. Last year, I was working for my dad. Now, if I'd try to see him—I love my father and family—I'd get a jackknife in my back from my brother-in-law. My father don't want it

71

that way, but he's living with his son-in-law and he has to go along.

"There's a Christmas spirit. The guys get a little drunk and that and they're able to forget about Christmas."

"Christmas Is Supposed to Be the Birth of Christ. If You're Poor at Christmas, Though, It Doesn't Mean Much."

I don't really know what I'd consider a good Christmas. My family was all killed when I was six years old. I was in the car at the time but I never got hurt. It was Labor Day 1946. I don't remember anything before that. I was only six years old.

"The first Christmas I got back from Viet Nam I just seemed to be glad I was back from over there. During Christmas there we had been given fresh turkey instead of C rations. This has been kind-of a rough year all around. I was working up to about two weeks before Thanksgiving and then I got laid off of a very good job.

"I'll say one thing. For me it's nothing tonight. I may play cards with a bunch of the fellas around here. Christmas is supposed to be the birth of Christ. If you're poor at Christmas, though, it doesn't mean much."

"I Can Never Understand Why They Have Christmas Parties for Lonely People a Week Before Christmas."

There are a lot of lonely people who spend their holidays in a room by themselves with only the memories of past Christmases which they enjoyed with their families which are now departed.

"A lot of groups and organizations have parties or dinners for these people, but I can never understand why they always have Christmas parties a week before the holiday. Why can't they have the dinner and entertainment on Christmas day, which is so lonesome for people. Some restaurant or organization could charge a certain amount and make a profit and make the last years for someone a little easier."

"I Gave All the Presents I Got for Christmas Back."

I gave all the gifts I got for Christmas back, and I didn't buy any. To me, there's nothing to it. I don't know why. It just doesn't turn me on. It's just another day.

"Thanks to my parents, I had to open them, because they were getting pissed off. But I didn't get anything I needed.

"I did get a pair of pajamas I needed so I'm keeping them, but like I got this big plastic chair that you blow-up. I think it's totally unnecessary.

"But here are all these people who need food and clothes, and you're supposed to take something you don't want just because people need to give it to you.

"You get all these perfumes and crap like that. Sure there's a thought behind it, but I dunno.

"I got a peace symbol necklace for Christmas, and I think they're hypocritical. Everybody's wearing them, and these same people you see fighting and arguing all the time. I mean, like what's it supposed to mean.

"I also got clothes. I have enough to wear and I don't need them.

"I don't know how Christmas ought to be celebrated. Maybe, I'm putting it down too much. Still, I don't see any sense to it. It seems like it's almost all for the middle class and it's a big advertising campaign.

"I didn't even want to spend Christmas with my family. I had no feeling. It was just dead, you know.

"I'm a junior in high school. I don't know if any other kids my age feel the way I do. I know a lot go along with it even though it's phoney.

"I'd rather not even have a tree, and I'd rather spend it alone or with my boyfriend even though I don't know that the holiday would be brought into it.

"Maybe, you ought to just create your own holidays when something happens.

"My family's very touchy. They ask me, 'Why don't you just tolerate Christmas?' "

"No Matter How You Explains to Children, They Keeps Looking for Things."

We lives in the projects and is on welfare. My husband, he been sick all this year. He had an accident, his pancreas went bad and he had his appendix out.

"Our checks come the end of the month. The little bit of money you get only enough for food and rent.

"The kids, they says they wants lots of things for Christmas. I tell 'em we go to church. I don't tells 'em about no Santa Claus. No matter how you explains to children, they keeps looking for things. They thinks you a genius to make something somehow.

"Still, we wouldna have Christmas, if it not for the birth of Christ."

"We know the savings are there; it's a matter of prying them loose."—Reese Williams, Mgr. of the shopping center, Quoted: Business Week Dec. 5, 1970

'It's Hard When You Can't Give."

I was sick last Christmas and my husband was out of work. The children only got what my Momma sent and what the church gave them.

"It's tough not to be able to give when you want to. It's better to give than to get, as the saying goes, and it's hard when you can't.

"We have it pretty hard this Christmas. My husband left and has been gone several months. We try to do the best we can and we're lucky if we get anything. This time our name was turned into the Salvation Army and they sent us a check for Christmas."

"You might call our units 'super juvenile stores.' They carry such an abundance of toys and related products, priced competitively, that the consumer is absolutely overwhelmed.

"Once that impression has been made, we strive to maintain a kind of pleasant atmosphere that makes shopping at Child World comfortable and enjoyable."—Sid Shneider, Pres., Child World, Inc. Quoted: "Toys", Nov. 1970

"Ya Cuts Down on Meats and Even Potatoes . . .to Buy Christmas."

I take from my food money to buy Christmas. I start around September and buy little things and put the stuff at my daughter's house.

"Ya cut down on meats and even on potatoes to do it. I buy the instant potatoes. They go farther.

"When I run out, I borrow. Most of the people I know are on welfare. We borrow back and forth and we don't owe nobody.

"Still, as far as Christmas last year went, it stunk. There's never enough money, never enough of anything. There's never even enough clothes.

"All this stuff you hear of given at Christmas through public aid for families, I never saw it."

"A Meager Christmas ...a Meatloaf."

Last year, we had a meager Christmas, but we did manage to have a meatloaf. I scrounged up $3 two years ago for an artificial tree. My kids are crying for a real one.

"Living on welfare is like hell. Your life is not your own. Seems like you're a puppet on a string. You have to answer for everything. If there's an extra pot on the stove, they want to know if it came from a boyfriend and you're not allowed to have any boyfriends.

"A boy gets in trouble and right away the cop says, 'The old lady's on welfare.' A mother can only do what she can afford.

"The rich society is very ignorant of the poor people. They don't even want to know they exist. The politicians say there is no hunger, but they don't go into the slums. You can't see how the people on welfare live by driving on Lake Shore Drive.

"I think Christmas is a good idea because it gives a few of the rich a chance to see how the poor live.

"A family of 12 I know only had a pot of rice and beans for Christmas. The father had been laid off just before Christmas. They went to the Salvation Army and were able to buy 7 toys there, only enough for the younger ones.

"I only wish those who have money could see the light in a poor child's eye when he get a toy."

**"PLAYBOY'S
CHRISTMAS
GIFT GUIDE** "peace on earth
and good-will offerings
for friends, lovers—or yourself

"Multilayer bronze relief, by Stephen Edlich,
$1400. AM—FM receiver that comes with a pair
of 360-degree orange speakers by Philco Ford,
$219.95. Battery-powered leap-year calendar
clock, by Actuelle, $175; and two adult puzzles of
removable lucite pieces that form abstract sculp-
tures, by Itemation, $7 each. Plexiglass and bronze
chess set with board, from Continuum, $150 . . ."

"Christmas I Always Remember as the Time of the Year When You Really Scrimp."

My mother and my brothers and sisters are on welfare. Christmas I always remember as the time of the year when you really scrimped.

"I remember way back the Salvation Army bringing boxes into our house. At the time I liked it. Later, it bothered me. Why were these people bringing these things?

"Christmas—that's when you can really distinguish the haves from the have-nots."

"Everyone at School Brags About What They Got for Christmas. Me, I Keep My Mouth Shut."

I'm 16 years old and we're on welfare. Lots of times at Christmas us kids did not get anything. My mother just did not have the money to buy it.

"Everyone at school brags about what they got for Christmas. Me, I keep my mouth shut.

"I'd love to have a maxi-coat. All the other kids have them. We get our stuff from the Salvation Army or we get it donated. You don't get anything very fancy that way.

"I'm lucky, though. They let us wear slacks at school."

"A group of angry fathers in Montreal put on Santa Claus outfits and held a street parade carrying such signs as 'Our Christmas—a big bill for everyone,' and I'm tired of playing Santa Claus, I can't even pay for all my gifts."—News Item

"I Use to Be Catholic and Go to Churches Christmas...Things Like That. But I Change My Mind."

I'm afraid tonight.

"I know what's going to be ... one Judge ... one God. I'm supposed to be a Catholic. But I got a girl friend. She's a honey. Don't forget I'm not a chicken see, I'm 72 years old and tonight I'm going to go to the over-30 club. I one of the finest waltzers in this country and Christmas is a big holiday.

"I use to be Catholic and go to churches Christmas ... things like that. But I change my mind. Today, everyday is change. From 1913 I'm in this country. Before, many years back, it could be happy. We use to go places and enjoy ourselves. There use to be place open day and night. Today I'm afraid to go on the bus. It happened to me twice. Once with a big knife. I say to him 'If you gonna follow me I gonna hollar.' I give him the B.S. line, tell him I gamble my money away. So I beat 'em twice like that. I'm a very lucky man.

"It use to be very good, very good. People laugh, they laugh, but now they are afraid. I'm afraid to walk the street tonight. No protection. No place to hide yourself. Before many years back it could be happy. But it happened to me twice. I'm afraid tonight."

"The Week Before Christmas, Well I Ain't Proud of It but We Were Stealing Our Food."

It was a pretty tight Christmas, but at least there was food in the house. The welfare finally gave us emergency food stamps.

"The week before Christmas, well I ain't proud of it, but we were stealing our food. I felt bad for doing it. I ain't a debased person, but my wife and I were hungry.

"We've taken food from the homes of people we were visiting. You know in a rural area like this, people usually have a lot in the freezer.

"Also, we've gone into a meat market with the explicit intent to steal and we've taken what meat we

93

needed for supper. We took what we needed and just what we needed. Someday, we hope to repay what we took, even though they don't know we took it.

"We knew we couldn't get welfare cuz there weren't no children. I got a good job. It pays good money, but it's working for a gravel company and they don't do no work once the ground freezes. I just got the job in August and I couldn't save no money cuz I owed it all to creditors.

"My wife's been sick since we got married 2 years ago. She works till she gets run down and then I make her quit.

"Nobody'll hire me around here cuz they know I work for the gravel company. It's that way with a lot of guys.

"The Waukegan Public Aid Department lady made it seem like it was all our fault. She said we had to go to our township supervisor, but we were told he was out and nobody knew when he was gonna be back. We were told we could go down to the public aid office in Waukegan at 7:30 in the morning and try to get food stamps. They only take so many and then just some of them get stamps. Well, we didn't have gas to put in the car for it.

"Finally, I called a newspaper and we got food stamps within two hours.

"It made Christmas a lot better. I went out in the woods we live by and chopped down a tree. It wasn't full like the kind you buy, but that was all right. We bought some popcorn out of the foodstamps and my wife strung it on the tree.

"We went over to my parents' house Christmas eve. We didn't exchange gifts cus they haven't got much either, but we brought a game we have and deck of cards and we just enjoyed being together.

"My wife's parents have 11 kids. She just made a picture of a butterfly for her mother and we borrowed some money from my folks and bought her dad a shirt for Christmas.

"A couple of days after Christmas I got an anonymous note from someone on the newspaper who had heard of our situation. It said that the man who was sending it had lost his wife within the last year and wasn't going to have too great of a Christmas either. He included two $5 bills, which he said he thought might help us a little. Man, that note was my Christmas present. I was given back a little of my faith in human nature."